Listen to your Mother, Dandelion

an "I believe in you" book

Written by Marietta Camps
Illustrated by Paula Mould

First Published in Ontario, Canada in 2018
by www.duo.ca
enquiries: ncamps@duo.ca
© 2018 Marietta Camps

Mother Dandelion looked at the dandelions, clover and buttercups growing around her in the field.

"I really don't belong here," she thought. "I should really be growing in a beautiful garden. And look at this grass, how coarse it is. Only good enough for cows! When the time comes, I am going to make sure that my children are going to do better than this. I shall have to think about this very seriously."

And while she thought and thought and thought, her petals closed up tight, and soon all she had left was a fluffy puff ball with seeds.

"Aha, now is my chance!" she thought, and she waited patiently for the wind to come along to help her.

She waited and waited and waited, but there was no wind, and one by one her seeds dropped into the meadow. And since she had refused to speak to the other dandelions that grew around her, they ignored her and went about their business of preparing for the next crop of dandelions.

Mother Dandelion held on to her last remaining seed, hoping that a gust of wind would soon come.

Just as she felt that she could not cling to her seed any longer, the grasses about her stirred with the first whisper of a breeze.

"Not yet, not yet," Mother Dandelion said, holding on tightly to the last seed, as she willed the wind to blow harder and harder.

The wind dove down and all the grasses, buttercups and dandelions danced like waves in the sea. Mother Dandelion waited until she felt it was the right moment.

With the next strong gust of wind she released her seed which went sailing over the meadow, over hedges and streams, over castles and villages further and further away from its parent who had given it strict instructions that it was only to settle down in the best of gardens.

"But what is the best of gardens?" asked the seedling nervously, as it was carried along with the wind.

The wind whistled over the ocean, it puffed and puffed as it climbed the highest mountains. It carried the seedling along with it over strange and wonderful lands, never stopping until it started to slow down over what seemed to be a vast, endless desert.

"Surely not here," moaned the seed, trailing its sadly drooping hairs as it surveyed the scene below.

The desert started showing a tree here and there, and then a few small houses and patches of green, but as far as the seed could see, no garden at all.

"And this is where I leave you," said the wind, which had been silent all this while.

The seed whirled and twirled down to the dry earth where it fell softly and gently to the ground at the edge of a village. But fortunately for the seedling, it landed close to a well which was guarded day and night because the water in it was more precious than gold.

The village women with their children would come and throw in a bucket and draw up the water and carefully pour the precious water into their leather pouches to take home. Of course, there were a few spills, and the water drops fell on the thirsty seedling sleeping in the hot earth.

Little by little, the seed became fatter and fatter until it burst open and out came the tiniest shoot which stretched up to the desert sun.

There were so many people and so many children, the growing Dandelion was in danger of being stepped on, until a little child noticed something green growing at his feet. He had never seen a Dandelion before and he called to his Mother. She, of course, called to the other women and they all stood around wondering what kind of plant this was.

"Could be bad," said one. "Let's dig it up and burn it."

"No," said others. "Let's see what it grows up to be and we can always dig it up then."

So the villagers took turns to water the Dandelion and on the hottest days, they even made a shade for it. The Dandelion grew and grew and its leaves were green and shiny. The tight bud in its centre grew bigger and to the delight of the villagers the Dandelion burst into yellow bloom.

"Aie, aie!" they called out to each other. "Did you ever see such beautiful yellow petals? This is indeed a magical flower!" and they sang and danced around the Dandelion, which proudly smiled upon them all.

"I am special, I am special after all, just as my Mother had wanted me to be!" sang the little dandelion.

That's not really the end of the story because one week later the dandelion had its own seeds and then there were more and more yellow flowers.

The villagers discovered something even more wonderful - for everything about the Dandelion could be used. From its roots for making teas and medicines, to its leaves in salads and its petals for making beautiful yellow dyes. Mother Dandelion had been right. It was special.

Happy Ending.

Why do people wish on dandelions?

The word "folklore" means beliefs and customs that are passed through time by telling, in songs and in stories. Folklore tells us that when people blow the seeds from a dandelion and make a wish, their wishes and thoughts may come true. People also wish on shooting stars in the night sky and on four-leaf clovers.

Some people believe that dandelions can tell what kind of weather is coming. When dandelions have turned to seeds, they will open into a full ball in good weather. If rain is on the way, however, they will fold like an umbrella and remain tightly closed.

Dandelion seeds are spread by wind (including when you blow on them), by water and by animals. A single dandelion plant has many seeds to be sure that at least a few will find a good place to land and grow. While dandelions are beautiful and have many purposes, most people do not want them growing in their lawn. Maybe one day, the dandelion will be loved by everyone.

Did you know?

Dandelions have been used by humans for food and as a helpful herb for much of recorded history.

A whole range of garden wildlife depends on dandelions for food, especially in the spring.

Seeds are light and have feathery bristles and can be carried long distances by the wind. This means it is hard to control where dandelions will grow.

The flower heads mature into a round seed head called lowballs. Each lowball has many single seeds attached to a pappus of fine hairs which help the seed to be airborne over long distances.

The plant requires as little as eight weeks to grow through the seedling stage and bloom. The bloom matures to seeds in as little as a week. Because it spreads so quickly, most people consider it to be a weed. Maybe not?

1. Draw your own version 'freehand' which means you look at our dandelion and draw your own version of it. Notice how our colours are blended or rubbed together, or...

2. You can photocopy or trace our dandelion and colour your copy or...

3. Why don't you write your own story about a dandelion or anything you want and draw pictures to go along with your story.

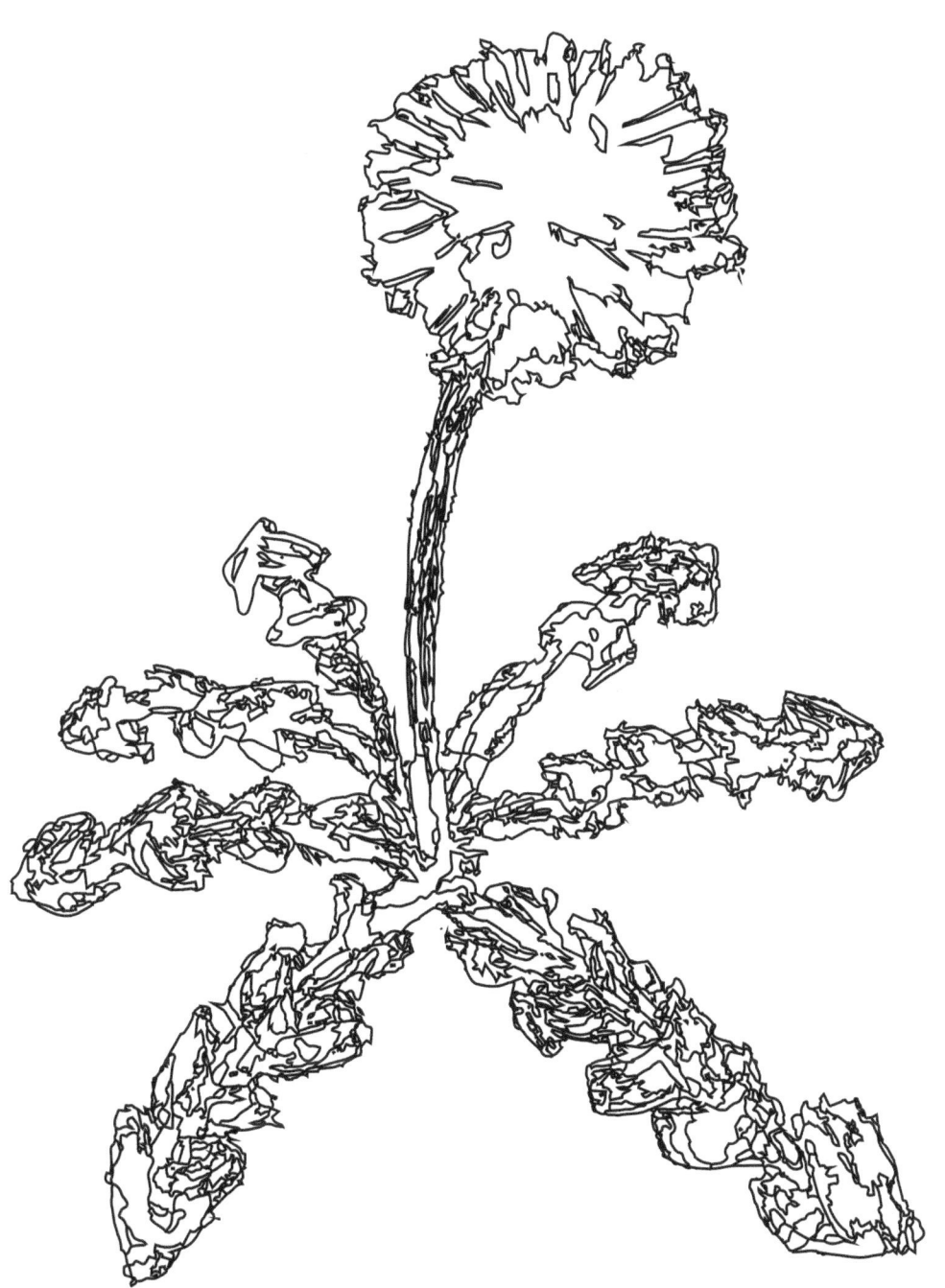

www.ingramcontent.com/pod-product-compliance
Lightning Source LLC
Chambersburg PA
CBHW041401160426
42811CB00101B/1509